High Hopes

170 Ways to Lift Your Spirits

Patrick Lindsay

MJF BOOKS
New York

Published by MJF Books
Fine Communications
322 Eighth Avenue
New York, NY 10001

High Hopes
LC Control Number: 2015957152
ISBN 978-1-60671-340-2

This edition is published by MJF Books in
arrangement with Lime Tree Books.

Designed by Lisa Chovnick

Printed in the United States of America.

MJF Books and the MJF colophon are trademarks
of Fine Creative Media, Inc.

QF   10   9   8   7   6   5   4   3   2

For Lisa, Nathan, Kate,
Sarah, Nic & Josh

Change Your Default Settings

LIKE DIGITAL devices, we start life on our
default settings. But that's operating at our most
basic level. To discover our true potential, we must
explore the outer limits of our settings. We're
works in progress, the possibilities are endless.

*The great majority of men are
bundles of beginnings.*

RALPH WALDO EMERSON (1803–1882)

Gather Mindful Moments

SLOW THE daily rush. Filter out past problems.
Take a childlike approach and recognize the
moment you're living. Savor it as it happens, rather
than looking to the next one.

*Every morning we are born again. What
we do today is what matters most.*

GAUTAMA BUDDHA (CA. 563–483 BC)

Give Kindness Freely

BESTOW KINDNESS wherever you can. Put no limits on it. Seek no response. Watch people's reactions. Give it especially to those who seem the most difficult. Often their responses are the most rewarding.

[The] best portion of a good man's life [is] his little, nameless, unremembered acts of kindness and of love.

WILLIAM WORDSWORTH (1770–1850)

Listen to Your Heart's Whispers

YOUR HEART is your true compass. But only if
you allow it to express itself freely, and only if
you listen to it. Sometimes it's barely audible,
whispering its real feelings. Listen for these,
they are often the most valuable.

Alas! There is no instinct like the heart.

LORD BYRON (1788–1824)

Meditate

LIKE DEFRAGGING your computer, meditation
clears your mind. It brings mindfulness and
encourages equilibrium. It promotes inner feelings
of calm and contentment. It broadens
your horizons.

All things are ready, if our minds be so.

WILLIAM SHAKESPEARE (1564–1616)
HENRY V (ACT 4, SCENE 3)

Value Your Time

THE SIMPLE reality is there isn't time for everything. We have no guarantees of how much time we have. So we must respect it. We must spend it wisely. Not working every waking hour, but living, loving and learning.

What would be the use of immortality to a person who cannot use well a half an hour?

RALPH WALDO EMERSON (1803–1882)

Control Your Body

BE AWARE of your posture. Move with purpose.
Speak with authority. Take your place proudly. Lift
your pace. Your mood will follow.

*What you do speaks so loudly that I
cannot hear what you said.*

RALPH WALDO EMERSON (1803–1882)

Fight Complexity

SIMPLE THINGS are usually the most interesting. And bigger isn't necessarily better. Life is at its best when it's at its simplest. Complexity can be suffocating. Fight against it. It's worth the crusade.

Simplicity is the ultimate sophistication.

LEONARDO DA VINCI (1452–1519)

Create Mind Pictures

ENVISAGE WHAT you want to achieve. Embed
your goals in your subconscious. They will act as a
silent compass, steering your decision making
and opening unseen doors on the path to
realizing them.

*Undoubtedly, we become
what we envisage.*

CLAUDE M. BRISTOL (1891–1951)

Find Your Style

RECOGNIZE AND develop your own style. Style always outlasts fashion. Make sure your style is authentic. Take advantage of your best attributes: your personality, your presence, your voice. Be comfortable with your style.

*Fashion is what you adopt when
you don't know who you are.*

QUENTIN CRISP (1908–1999)

Have a Mind-Lift

FORGET ABOUT face-lifts, look deeper than that. Give yourself a mind-lift. Work on improving your brainpower. The options are many: read voraciously, play mental games, do puzzles. Change your perspective, look at other viewpoints.

The mind is everything. What you think, you become.

GAUTAMA BUDDHA (CA. 563–483 BC)

Write Your Lifeline

CHART YOUR achievements. Give credit where it's due. Place your life in its true perspective. Take confidence from your successes. Learn from your failures. Aim for your goals.

Not until we are lost do we begin to understand ourselves.

HENRY DAVID THOREAU (1817–1862)

Die Young, but Live Long

As WE age we need regular mental software
updates. There may be some hardware glitches,
but updates can overcome most of them. Turn
newer with each day as you seek knowledge and
new experiences. Remember, if you
don't use it (. . . *you lose it*)

It takes a long time to become young.

PABLO PICASSO (1881–1973)

Develop Focus

ABOVE ALL, focus is the key to progress. Without it, your skills and attributes are diluted. With it, they are magnified and intensified. Focus sets you apart from the also-rans. It enables you to see through obstacles. It clears the path to your goal.

If you run after two hares,
you will catch neither.

THOMAS FULLER (1608–1661)

Know Your Own Secrets

BE BRUTALLY honest with yourself. Only you
know your innermost secrets. They can be a
positive or negative force, depending on how you
treat them. Turn them into positives by taking
responsibility for them.

*Everyone is a moon, and has a dark side
which he never shows to anybody.*

MARK TWAIN (SAMUEL LANGHORNE CLEMENS)
(1835–1910)

Embrace Your Humanity

IT'S WHAT sets you apart. It's centered on your view of the world. Make sure it's genuine, that it's yours. Ensure you're not copying someone else's views. When you're confident in your beliefs, build on them, stay true to them.

The privilege of a lifetime is to become who you truly are.

CARL JUNG (1875–1961)

Look Inside

IGNORE THE external forces surrounding you.
The answers to our deepest questions lie inside us.
Here, you are in control. You can choose your
direction. You can listen to your inner voice. You
make your choices.

This above all: to thine own self be true.

WILLIAM SHAKESPEARE (1564–1616)
HAMLET (ACT 1, SCENE 3)

Withhold Judgment

IT'S SO easy to become a critic . . . after all,
you need no qualifications. Resist the temptation to
join the naysayers. Take the positive road. Look for
the light. And, if something is wrong, consider
how to fix it.

Don't find fault. Find a remedy.

HENRY FORD (1863–1947)

Embrace Your Flaws

PERFECTION EXISTS only in our dreams.
In real life it's unattainable and often unattractive.
Our imperfections set us apart as much as our
achievements. Once we learn to accept them,
we gain confidence . . . in our strengths, our
resilience and our potential. After all, if we
reach perfection, there's only one way to go.

Certain flaws are necessary for the whole.
It would seem strange if old friends
lacked certain quirks.

JOHANN WOLFGANG VON GOETHE (1749–1832)

Count Your Blessings

THE MORE we're thankful for what we've got,
the more we realize just how much we have. Most
of us are so far ahead of the game . . . family, loved
ones, friends, lifestyle, nature . . . shortcomings in
one are usually made up in others. Look
around in gratitude.

All which we behold is full of blessings.

WILLIAM WORDSWORTH (1770–1850)

Greet the Dawn

EVERY DAY welcomes you with opportunity. It's a blank canvas awaiting your paintbrush. With the dawn comes renewed hope. Face it with relish. Feel its warming embrace. Let its growing energy recharge you.

*The sun has not caught me
in bed in fifty years.*

THOMAS JEFFERSON (1743–1826)

Downsize and Declutter

FEW ACTIVITIES are more empowering . . .
than ruthlessly pruning accumulated possessions.
Few of us need the things or the space we acquire.
Retain the essential, and those with special
meaning. Make the rest justify their retention . . .
or give them away. You'll be invigorated
beyond your expectations.

*It is preoccupation with possessions, more
than anything else, that prevents men
from living freely and nobly.*

BERTRAND RUSSELL (1872–1970)

Come Home to Yourself

ALL THE knowledge you acquire is available to
others. What sets you apart is how you use it.
Nobody has your unique combination of heart
and mind. At the end of each day, be content to be
you. From that foundation you can build . . .
a better you and a happier you.

*No one remains quite what he was
when he recognizes himself.*

THOMAS MANN (1875–1955)

Listen to What's Not Being Said

MOST OF us hear people speaking. What's
more important is what they're not saying. Look
for the subtext. Be aware of what has been left out.
Observe their revealing physical reactions. Often
the real message is in the omissions.

*The art of being wise is the art of
knowing what to overlook.*

WILLIAM JAMES (1842–1910)

Customs versus Laws

WHAT ARE presented as tried and tested
laws may simply be long-held unchallenged
customs. Many don't stand the test
of objective scrutiny. They often serve as
the basis for other assumptions. When
successfully demystified . . . they can
open unexpected pathways.

*Pardon him . . . [for he] thinks that
the customs of his tribe . . . are the
laws of nature.*

GEORGE BERNARD SHAW (1856–1950)
CAESAR AND CLEOPATRA, ACT 2

Learn Your Strengths

JUST AS others have to earn your respect,
so you have to earn self-respect. One way is to
honestly assess your strong points. We all have
them and they usually outweigh our weaknesses.
Take the time to isolate your strengths.
Then use them wisely.

He who knows others is learned.
He who knows himself is wise.

LAO-TZU (604–531 BC)

Slow Your Eating

ONE OF the best places to start savoring life . . . is during your meals. Stop thinking of food as fuel . . . or worse, as comfort. Eat slowly . . . enjoy the taste, digest better, lose stress . . . and weight.

There is more to life than increasing its speed.

MOHANDAS KARAMCHAND "MAHATMA" GANDHI (1869–1948)

Live Now

REFUSE TO let time dictate your day. Lose track of it. Immerse yourself in whatever you're doing. Surrender yourself to the activity. Commit your full attention. Notice the difference.

The happiest of all lives is a busy solitude.

VOLTAIRE (FRANÇOIS-MARIE AROUET) (1694-1778)

Think for Yourself

IT SOUNDS so obvious . . . but look around and listen. Many people's thoughts are not their own. Many are recording machines on playback. Consider your opinions before you air them. Make sure you truly hold the viewpoint. Then you can deliver it with passion.

To find yourself, think for yourself.

SOCRATES (469–399 BC)

Seek Experiences

IT'S NOT about the experiences themselves . . .
but, rather, how you use them. And not only are
your experiences valuable. You can learn much
from others' experiences, and especially from
their mistakes. It can save a lot of pain.

*Learning is experience. Everything
else is just information.*

ALBERT EINSTEIN (1879–1955)

Light Up Your Life

WE CAN live in shadow or in light. We can choose to live in monochrome or Technicolor. Light comes from your heart. It shines through the darkness. It acts as a beacon, drawing others to you. Watch as they bask in it.

When you possess light within,
you see it externally.

ANAÏS NIN (1903–1977)

Evade the Gatekeepers

MUCH THAT is valuable is obscured by life's gatekeepers. These sentinels will try to deny you entry. They see it as their duty to preserve the status quo. To reach your goal you'll have to outwit them. If you're determined enough, you'll do it. Consider it the first step toward your target.

Arriving at one goal is the starting point to another.

JOHN DEWEY (1859–1952)

Stretch

DON'T SETTLE for comfortable. Push
yourself into the zone of uncertainty. Find the
challenges that will test you. Find the satisfaction
of achieving. You'll answer many questions about
yourself . . . questions that otherwise
remain dormant.

*One may go a long way
after one is tired.*

FRENCH PROVERB

Ignore the Frames

WHY BE limited by the frames others put
around you? Don't allow your vision to be
cropped. Don't allow someone else to edit your
dream. Others don't know your limitless
potential. They are hampered by their
preconceptions. Only you can
see the full picture.

---

*Is life not a hundred times too short
for us—to bore ourselves?*

FRIEDRICH NIETZSCHE (1844–1900)

Imagination Rules

LOOK AT the stories behind Apple or
Google. What imaginations envisaged them!
What perseverance brought them to fruition! Only
those giving their minds full reign achieve great
things. Your imagination is your greatest untapped
asset; it holds new worlds to conquer.

*Imagination is the highest
form of research.*

ALBERT EINSTEIN (1879–1955)

Look for the Pattern

MOST SITUATIONS develop to a pattern. It
may be camouflaged, or slow to reveal, but it's
usually there, and usually decipherable.
Understanding the patterns gives you power
to anticipate the next steps, or to break
the pattern to find novel solutions.

Habit rules the unreflecting herd.

WILLIAM WORDSWORTH (1770–1850)

Know Your Tribe

IT DOESN'T matter what you call it: a network;
support group; family; clan; tribe. We all need love,
support, a haven. In the worst of times, they are
there. Your tribe will forgive you. They'll
accept you and sustain you.

*Are we not two volumes
of the same book?*

MARCELINE DESBORDES-VALMORE (1786–1859)

Find Your Faith

DON'T FOLLOW blindly. Look up, look
around, observe consequences. Filter according
to your heart and common sense. Seek articles of
faith in which you'll find deep comfort. These are
your values. Visit them often, explore
them in depth.

*What matters is not the idea a man holds,
but the depth at which he holds it.*

EZRA POUND (1885–1972)

Move to Trash

IF YOU'VE proved that an idea or belief lacks
merit, jettison it without remorse. Don't hold on to
it from habit. We never stand still. Our ideas grow
and change as we do. Keep questioning
and growing.

*The only man I know who behaves sensibly
is my tailor; he takes my measurements anew
each time he sees me. The rest go on with
their old measurements and expect
me to fit them.*

GEORGE BERNARD SHAW (1856–1950)

Work in the Crevices

THE WORLD never fits together perfectly. There are always gaps. Often they are windows of opportunity. Shine a light into the crevices. Work in there, somewhere between conformity and chaos. Great rewards reside there.

Vision is the art of seeing things invisible.

JONATHAN SWIFT (1667–1745)

Get Street-Smart

THERE'S study-smart and street-smart. There's education and self-education. The ideal is a combination of the two. One without the other ultimately brings limitations. But, if you have to choose, err on the side of the street.

*A child educated only at school
is an uneducated child.*

GEORGE SANTAYANA (1863–1952)

Create

OUR CREATIVITY is our endless source of
energy. It opens our mind's eye and fuels our
adventures. It travels with us and lifts our spirits.
It constantly duels with our better judgment.
Give your creative side a chance to thrive.
Encourage it every time it sparks.

*The question is not what you
look at, but what you see.*

HENRY DAVID THOREAU (1817–1862)

Who Are You?

IT'S AN intriguing question . . . but perhaps not the most important one. The crucial one is: what might I become? To know that, you need to know yourself. And that is a gradual process, because we are ever changing.

When I let go of what I am,
I become what I might be.

LAO-TZU (604–531 BC)

Mind the Media

OUR FORMATIVE media bear little
resemblance to our children's. Once it was
radio, TV, music, film, newspapers, magazines,
comics. Now it's the Internet, social media, apps,
games, etc. Messages used to travel vertically. Now
they move horizontally . . . and parents
are often the link that's cut out.

*Respect your parents; they
pay for your Internet.*

ANONYMOUS

Lose the Pretense

WE ARE only truly content as our authentic
selves. We wear our pretenses for protection,
or because we fear we won't fit in. They are
temporary disguises that usually mask our
better, real, selves. Reveal the genuine
you and embrace it.

*We become so accustomed to
disguise ourselves to others that at last
we are disguised to ourselves.*

FRANÇOIS VI, DUC DE LA ROCHEFOUCAULD
(1613–1680)

Your Eyes Have It

YOUR DIGITAL camera has nothing on your eye.
Top cameras may have 20 megapixels. Your retina
has about 576 megapixels! Buying a camera doesn't
make you a great photographer. It only makes
you a camera owner. Use your eyes like
a great photographer.

*The most pathetic person in the world is
someone who has sight but no vision.*

HELEN KELLER (1880–1968)

Read the Signs

NOT THE obvious signs; read the subliminal ones. Poker players call them "tells": physical signals revealing true intentions, intentions often contradicting the words uttered. Develop your skills by constant observation. It will pay great dividends.

[*The*] *power of accurate observation . . .*
is commonly called cynicism by those
who have not got it.

GEORGE BERNARD SHAW (1856–1950)

Do a Google Search

TAKE THE Google approach: carefully examine your options, prioritize them, filter them by credibility and importance, then chart your course. Wisdom is using experience to choose.

Life is the sum of all your choices.

ALBERT CAMUS (1913–1960)

Travel Firsthand

WHEN MAKING your decisions . . . rely on
primary sources or firsthand experience, not on
others' views. That way, at least you make your
own mistakes. You don't blindly replicate
those made by others.

*Trust yourself. You know more
than you think you do.*

DR. BENJAMIN SPOCK (1903–1998)

Customize Yourself

YOU HAVEN'T come off an assembly line.
You're a unique customized model. Refuse to be
defined by the labels they stick on you. Insist on
being the top of the line. And that means
adjusting to changing circumstances.
But never fear the upgrade.

~

*The secret of change is to focus all of
your energy, not on fighting the old,
but on building the new.*

DAN MILLMAN (B. 1946)

Lose the Self-Pity

IF WE stop being self-centered, we change our
viewpoint on everything. We widen our horizons,
we start thinking about others instead of ourselves.
We break away from a strangling negativity. We
form a solid positive base.

*Self-pity is our worst enemy and if we
yield to it, we can never do anything
wise in this world.*

HELEN KELLER (1880–1968)

Prepare

HOW OFTEN have we seen chances go begging, simply because we weren't ready to take advantage of them? Clearly we can't prepare for every eventuality, but common sense will show us most of them. Whenever you can, think ahead. Prepare and be ahead of the game.

*He who is best prepared can best
serve his moment of inspiration.*

SAMUEL TAYLOR COLERIDGE (1772–1834)

Don't Do Shy

SHYNESS SIMPLY isn't worth it. It's based on a
misapprehension: that others find what we do, or
how we look, important. Most of us are hit by
shyness at some times in our lives. But do
everything you can to overcome it. It
makes you miss out on too much.

The shell must break before
the bird can fly.

ALFRED, LORD TENNYSON (1809–1892)

Shine

DON'T JUST go through the motions.
Whatever you do, make it really worthwhile.
Stretch yourself, ignite your passions, put your
heart and soul into it. The resulting energy
will transform you. And it will radiate
to those around you.

*Some people are so much
sunshine to the square inch.*

WALT WHITMAN (1819–1892)

Take Time

FIGHT AGAINST the urge to rush. Savor experiences, explore their meanings, learn from them. Take the time to register your feelings. Turn experience into wisdom.

To live is to be slowly born.

ANTOINE DE SAINT-EXUPÉRY (1900–1944)

Use Your Own Typeface

EACH OF us has our own unique typeface . . .
our handwriting. It's almost as distinctive as our
fingerprints. Don't waste it, be proud of it, use it
often. Send handwritten letters and notes to friends
and loved ones. Each one is a special gift.

Beauty is God's handwriting—
a wayside sacrament.

CHARLES KINGSLEY (1819–1875)

Make Peace with the Past

COME TO terms with the past. Learn from it.
Use it like a guidebook for the future. But don't
get bogged down in analyzing it. Visit it every so
often to draw wisdom from it. But by no
means live there.

*Don't let yesterday use up
too much of today.*

CHEROKEE PROVERB

Play with Your Pet

IT'S GUARANTEED to improve your mood. It's scientifically proven! Even playing with someone else's pet will work. Take your dog for a walk . . . and spread the cheer to others. Do it every day.

Until one has loved an animal, a part of one's soul remains unawakened.

ANATOLE FRANCE (1844–1924)

Spend Time with a Close Friend

IT'S BETTER than any medicine, and works
like a human antidepressant. The familiarity, the
shared memories, will warm your heart and
spark laughter. Friends link us to our past,
and guide us into the future.

Friendship is a sheltering tree.

SAMUEL TAYLOR COLERIDGE (1772–1834)

Look Ahead

DON'T VIEW life through a rearview mirror,
don't second-guess or recriminate. Keep your gaze
forward. Look with anticipation, with optimism,
untrammeled by the baggage of the past.

*There are far, far better things ahead
than any we leave behind.*

C. S. LEWIS (1898–1963)

Be a Generalist

OUR SOCIETY glorifies the experts.
And certainly they have their place. But let's give
some credit to those with the wide view. Let's
support the all-arounders, and appreciate their
breadth of knowledge. Let's strive for
a balanced approach.

*There is nothing so stupid as the
educated man, if you get him off
the thing he was educated in.*

WILL ROGERS (1879–1935)

Savor the Scents

THEY ARE redolent of our lives' enduring memories. Each brings back images flash-frozen in our minds. The flowers, the trees, the ocean, the perfumes, the aftershaves. Welcome them back. Revel in them.

Pleasure is the flower that passes;
remembrance, the lasting perfume.

STANISLAS-JEAN, CHEVALIER DE BOUFFLERS
(1738–1815)

Sing Your Own Song

CREATE YOUR own melodies. Write your
own lyrics. Draw them from your feelings and
experiences. Sing from the heart. But make
sure it's original . . . cover bands have
little influence on the world.

*A bird does not sing because it has an
answer. It sings because it has a song.*

CHINESE PROVERB

Seek Beginnings

EACH TIME something ends, another thing starts. So ignore the endings. Focus on the new paths that open. And treasure your first-time experiences. They can't be repeated, no matter how hard you try.

A person often meets his destiny on the road he took to avoid it.

JEAN DE LA FONTAINE (1621–1695)

Get More Sleep

MAKE SURE you allow your body to recover and repair. Sleep deprivation has many negative impacts: it dulls recall of the good times, and enhances recall of the bad ones. Sleep well, wake up positive, and look forward to the day ahead.

Fatigue is the best pillow.

BENJAMIN FRANKLIN (1706–1790)

Find Fresh Air

BREAK OUT of the boxes where you live and work. Walk, sit, observe, suck in the air. Feel the breeze move around you. Watch the birds soar through it, and the trees bend to it. Even twenty minutes of fresh air will lift your mood.

When you arise in the morning, think what a precious privilege it is to be alive—to breathe, to think, to enjoy, to love.

MARCUS AURELIUS (121–180)

Impress Yourself

IN THE end, there's only one person who can judge, only one who knows your true thoughts and feelings . . . you. Forget about living up to others' expectations. Create your own expectations, and live up to them.

At the center of your being you have the answer; you know who you are and you know what you want.

LAO-TZU (604–531 BC)

Enjoy Growing Older

AS WE get older good things happen.
We become less judgmental. We filter out
negativity. We emphasize the positive. We
value the days. We appreciate life.

There is an unspeakable dawn
in happy old age.

VICTOR HUGO (1802–1885)

Be a Great Memory

ENJOY EVERY moment with your friends
and family. Don't hold back with your loved
ones. There are no guarantees on how long we
have together. Make your time here count. In
the end, all we leave is love and memories.
Make sure you leave behind great memories.

*Memory . . . is the diary that
we all carry about with us.*

OSCAR WILDE (1854–1900)

Cut the Commute

IF THERE'S any way you can, lose the commute.
The long, grinding, wasted hours take their toll.
But if you're locked into a long journey to work,
do everything you can to enliven it. Just don't get
so enmeshed in technology that you can't
appreciate the passing world.

Only dead fish swim with the stream.

MALCOLM MUGGERIDGE (1903–1990)

Don't Magnify

TREAT PROBLEMS or triumphs with the respect they deserve. But no more. Don't make them bigger than they are. Discern the real from the perceived. Keep them in perspective. View with a healthy skepticism.

Believe nothing, no matter where you read it, or who said it—even if I have said it— unless it agrees with your own reason and your own common sense.

GAUTAMA BUDDHA (CA. 563–483 BC)

Give Others a Break

TRY NOT to be such a hard marker. Allow
for the vagaries of others . . . their unknown
personal problems. Give them the benefit of the
doubt. Make allowances for others . . .
and yourself.

*It often happens that a man is more
humanely related to a cat or dog than
to any human being.*

HENRY DAVID THOREAU (1817–1862)

One Thing at a Time

MULTITASKING is greatly overrated. It can dissipate your efforts and cut your concentration span. Do it when you must. But when you can, focus all your energies on the task at hand.

The sun's rays do not burn until brought to a focus.

ALEXANDER GRAHAM BELL (1847–1922)

Take the Lead

WHEN YOU know you're the right person,
don't wait for approval, stand up and show the
way. Lead by example. Encourage others.
Blaze the trail.

~~~~~

Example is not the main *thing in
influencing others. It is the* only *thing.*

ALBERT SCHWEITZER (1875–1965)

Be Brave

YOU DON'T have to be movie brave, or war brave. It's often just acting because you know it's right, even though you're scared. When you follow your heart, it's surprising how you find courage you had no idea you possessed.

Each [man] is strong, relying on his own, and each is betrayed when he seeks in himself the courage of others.

RALPH WALDO EMERSON (1803–1882)

Use a Plate

HAVE A proper lunch. Don't just stuff fuel into your mouth. Take some time out. Detach from the grind. Dine. You'll return to work renewed.

We should look for someone to eat and drink with before looking for something to eat and drink.

EPICURUS (341–270 BC)

Live Your Truth

MOLD YOUR life around your beliefs, not the
other way around. Lose your preconceptions, and
your truth will emerge. Live your own truth,
not someone else's truth.

⌒

There is no god higher than truth.

MOHANDAS KARAMCHAND "MAHATMA" GANDHI
(1869–1948)

Reminisce

RECONNECT WITH old friends. Revisit old haunts. Rediscover old photos and letters. Bask in the warmth of the recollections. Let the laughter flow. Feel the spark of your spirit ignite.

*Things that were hard to bear
are sweet in the memory.*

LUCIUS ANNAEUS SENECA (4 BC–AD 65)

Watch People

OBSERVE THOSE you meet. Be curious.
Look past the first impressions. Take note
of the little details. Learn from them.
That's where wisdom lies.

Never trust to general impressions, my boy,
but concentrate yourself upon details.

ARTHUR CONAN DOYLE (1859–1930)

Look for the Growth

IT MAY not seem so at first, but the darkest days
often provide great opportunities. Among the
negativity and the turmoil, there will be hidden
moments. Look for them. They are chances
for growth, for love and forgiveness.

*A man must make his opportunity
as oft as find it.*

FRANCIS BACON (1561–1626)

Exercise

IT'S ONE of the best ways to lift your spirits.
Walk, run, swim, play sports, go to the gym . . .
get your blood pumping, let your endorphins flow.
They'll promote positive thoughts and
change your day's trajectory.

The first wealth is health.

RALPH WALDO EMERSON (1803–1882)

Use Your Tiredness

IT'S counterintuitive but it works in practice: try working when you're really weary. If you're a morning person, challenge problems at the end of your day. Your normal preconceptions will be less rigid. And often your brain will be more creative.

Dwell not on thy weariness, thy strength shall be according to the measure of thy desire.

ARAB PROVERB

Have a Chat

MAKE A new connection, or renew an
old one . . . a friend, family member, workmate,
stranger. Learn about them, hear about their
day. Listen to their problems. Put your
problems into perspective.

*The most fruitful and natural exercise of
the mind, in my opinion, is conversation.*

MICHEL DE MONTAIGNE (1533–1592)

Rise with the Sun

SYNCHRONIZE WITH nature. Wake with the
sun, without a jarring alarm. You create so many
extra hours in your day . . . the golden hours,
some of the most beautiful, often stressless,
hours in the day. It's the best time for
reflection or preparation.

The sun is but a morning star.

HENRY DAVID THOREAU (1817–1862)

Hold Your Dreams Tight

WHAT SETS apart those who achieve their
dreams, and those who don't? Persistence.
Refuse to give up on your dreams. You may
have to put them on hold sometimes.
But never abandon them.

*While he lives, he must think; while
he thinks, he must dream.*

ISAAC ASIMOV (1920–1992)

Ignore the Inconsequential

FORGET ABOUT annoying people, unimportant things, and small-minded opponents. Adjust your mind higher. Save your energies. Focus on things that truly matter.

Things that matter most must never be at the mercy of things that matter least.

JOHANN WOLFGANG VON GOETHE (1749–1832)

Be Mindful

MINDFULNESS HAS been with us for millennia. The ancients sought it through Buddhism. Now the Western world is embracing it. Even conservative medicine is adapting it. Develop your own way of mindfulness. Focus on the present without judgment.

Be happy in the moment, that's enough.
Each moment is all we need, not more.

MOTHER TERESA (ANJEZË GONXHE BOJAXHIU)
(1910–1997)

Be Thankful

WE SHOULD be grateful for so many things.
Yet often we take them for granted. Create a
routine of thanking people. Write to them
personally, especially letters. Let them know
your true feelings. It will bring
deep satisfaction.

～

*Gratitude bestows reverence, changing
forever how we experience
life and the world.*

JOHN MILTON (1608–1674)

Change Your Colors

COLORS CAN affect our moods, often
subtly and unconsciously. Each of us is affected
differently. Notice which colors bring you calmness,
and which stimulate. Surround yourself with those
that bring you peace.

*Color is my day-long obsession,
joy and torment.*

CLAUDE MONET (1840–1926)

Inspire Yourself

YOU CAN hardly expect to win others to your side
if you haven't inspired yourself. Sometimes
inspiration comes unbidden. Often you'll have to
chase it down. It's the spark that fires your
imagination. It's the dream that begets the goal.

I dream my painting,
and then I paint my dream.

VINCENT VAN GOGH (1853–1890)

Don't Hold Back

FAILING TO express our real feelings can lead
to profound regret. We usually hold back out of
fear, or to avoid hurting others' feelings. But
judiciously speaking from the heart leads
to deeper, more authentic connections.

You have enemies? Why, it is the
story of every man who has done a
great deed or created a new idea.

VICTOR HUGO (1802–1885)

Be Comfortable with Yourself

ABOVE ALL, accept your real self. Recognize
your weaknesses and work on them. But also
appreciate your strengths, your differences, your
idiosyncrasies. Aim to be centered,
not self-centered.

Style is knowing who you are, what you
want to say, and not giving a damn.

GORE VIDAL (1925–2012)

Don't Just Survive, Thrive

WE WRITE our own life stories. We can
stay in the wings, and play an "extra," or we can
write a leading role for ourselves. We can
leave our potential dormant, or we can
find greatness that lies within us.

*If one advances confidently in the
direction of his dreams, and endeavors to
live the life which he has imagined, he will
meet with a success unexpected in
common hours.*

HENRY DAVID THOREAU (1817–1862)

Be the Strength

DON'T LOOK for strength elsewhere . . . be it
yourself! Be the rock on which you, and others, rely.
Realize your potential by rising to the occasion.
Don't fear failure. Just making the effort will
win you great respect.

Freedom lies in being bold.

ROBERT FROST (1874–1963)

Look Pressure in the Eye

TRY TO take out the emotion. View the situation dispassionately, for what it is. Look for ways to ease the pressure. Set tasks, break them into manageable segments. That way your vision will be clear.

~

Our lamps were taken from us . . . and, on looking upwards, I saw . . . the night heaven thick with stars.

RALPH WALDO EMERSON (1803–1882)

Record Your Parents' Lives

YOU'LL HONOR them with your interest. And provide a great legacy for your children. You'll understand so much more about yourself. You'll be amazed at the things you didn't know, and surprised at their achievements. Your respect for them will soar.

When I was a boy of 14, my father was so ignorant I could hardly stand to have the old man around. But when I got to be 21, I was astonished at how much the old man had learned in seven years.

MARK TWAIN (SAMUEL LANGHORNE CLEMENS)

(1835–1910)

Go Natural

YOU KNOW it makes sense. Seek balance with your diet: organic, unprocessed food, natural fibers, etc. Go easy on—or lose—the alcohol. Look for nutrition suited to your age. Make sure your body's fuel is Premium.

*Let food be thy medicine and
medicine be thy food.*

HIPPOCRATES (460–377 BC)

Play On

ALWAYS FOSTER your competitive spirit. Keep playing games—physical and mental. From walking and swimming to ball games, to chess or cards or mind games. Try to excel according to your skill or your age. Set your own goals and go for them.

*Excitement is impossible where
there is no contest.*

HENRY CABOT LODGE JR. (1902–1985)

Wear Something You Love

YOUR FAVORITE clothes have a special aura.
They are impregnated with your memories. They
fold casually around your body. They bring
comfort. They bring familiarity and security.
They make you feel yourself.

*Know, first, who you are; and then
adorn yourself accordingly.*

EPICTETUS (55–135)

Explore Your Creativity

DON'T ACCEPT your perceptions of your
boundaries. They're often formed by misguided
experiences. Ignore them. Look at yourself afresh.
Ask: why not? Explore fresh fields.

*It is our duty as men and women
to proceed as though the limits of
our abilities do not exist.*

PIERRE TEILHARD DE CHARDIN, SJ (1881–1955)

Treasure Private Time

CREATE YOUR own cocoon, a haven without interruptions or distractions. Transport your mind and spirit there. Do nothing. Allow your mind to roam free. Gain perspective.

I will prepare and some day my chance will come.

ABRAHAM LINCOLN (1809–1865)

Carry Happiness

SHARE THE warmth of your happiness. Spread your smile. It's your gift. You worked for it, you own it. Give it freely. Others will reciprocate.

Let us be grateful to the people who make us happy; they are the charming gardeners who make our souls blossom.

MARCEL PROUST (1871–1922)

Begin Now

OUR LIVES are not eternal. Don't wait for some
magic sign. The sign is that you are here, and your
time starts now. Work toward your dreams,
your goals, one step at a time.

The future depends on what you do today.

MOHANDAS KARAMCHAND "MAHATMA" GANDHI
(1869–1948)

Acquire a New Skill

IT DOESN'T matter what it is, as long as
you're passionate about it. Open yourself to the
exploration. Push through the initial learning
stage. Absorb the knowledge with relish.
Enjoy the satisfaction of accomplishment.

Whatever you are, be a good one.

ABRAHAM LINCOLN (1809–1865)

Use Your Enthusiasm

IT'S THE catalyst . . . to ignite your spirit, put a
skip in your step, and a sparkle in your eye. It's
infectious. It contains a special magic.

There are only two ways to live your life.
One is as though nothing is a miracle. The
other is as though everything is a miracle.

ALBERT EINSTEIN (1879–1955)

Embrace the Wrinkles

IS THERE anything more soulless than the Botox look? Accept the wisdom lines, and the gray or thinning hair. Weave them in with your memories. Take charge as you journey into the Third Age. Go with pride and optimism.

Experience is one thing you can't get for nothing.

OSCAR WILDE (1854–1900)

Keep Your Word

RESPECT FLOWS to those whose word is
sacrosanct. Always honor your promises, even if it
brings disadvantage to you. Think carefully before
you commit your word. Ensure that you can deliver
on it. Once you give it, always keep it.

*It is not the oath that makes us believe
the man, but the man the oath.*

AESCHYLUS (525–456 BC)

Make Something

USE YOUR hands to make something tangible. Do it with love and passion. Paint, draw, build a table . . . whatever it is, put your heart into it. And when it's finished, give it away with love.

The only gift is a portion of thyself.

RALPH WALDO EMERSON (1803–1882)

Evolve

FLOW WITH technological changes. Don't slavishly follow every trend; rather, stay flexible and take a wide view. Look at the broad trends and adapt to them. Pick those that will allow you to maintain connections, especially with your friends, families, and colleagues.

Anyone who stops learning is old,
whether at twenty or eighty.

HENRY FORD (1863–1947)

Take a Child to the Zoo

EXPLORE WITH them. Feel their squealing
delight as you open up new worlds of imagination
and awe. Be their guide as they ask the
unanswerable questions. Delight in
their potential.

Wonder is the beginning of reason.

GREEK PROVERB

Share Love

DO IT without conditions, without boundaries.
Spread it around your family, your loved ones, even
your workmates. Sow the seeds . . . which will
flower down the years and leave a legacy.

Who, being loved, is poor?

OSCAR WILDE (1854–1900)

Travel

EXPLORE AND learn about . . . your suburb, your town, your country, your world. Keep your sense of adventure alive. Broaden your horizons, your knowledge, your interests.

*One's destination is never a place,
but a new way of seeing things.*

HENRY MILLER (1891–1980)

Take Responsibility

NOT JUST for your mistakes and failures, but also for your successes, and the problems that beset you. They may not be your fault, but it's your responsibility to react to them, to find solutions, to change things.

The price of greatness is responsibility.

WINSTON CHURCHILL (1874–1965)

Treasure Your Time

OUR TIME is a nonrenewable resource.
We each have a limited supply, in our days, in
our lives. Treat it with respect, prioritize its use.
Relish each minute. Spend time wisely.

*Tomorrow is a new day; you shall begin it
serenely and with too high a spirit to be
encumbered with your old nonsense.*

RALPH WALDO EMERSON (1803–1882)

Find the Fun

AT HOME or at work, always try to find humor.
Even in the toughest, busiest moments, lighten the
work with enjoyment. Keep things in perspective.
Keep the sparkle in your eyes. A smile will
brighten the day, and it's infectious.

*The most wasted of all days
is one without laughter.*

E. E. CUMMINGS (1894–1962)

Look Ahead

DON'T WASTE precious energy on past failures.
Learn the lessons. Apply them. But move on from
them. Keep your focus on the future, and the
endless potential and possibilities it offers.

And in today already walks tomorrow.

SAMUEL TAYLOR COLERIDGE (1772–1834)

Read, Don't Scan

TREAT GOOD writing with the respect it deserves. It's fine dining for the mind, not the fast food of social media or the Internet. Slow reading, like the slow-food movement, brings out the richness of the craft, and sets our imaginations alight.

Show me a family of readers and I will show you the people who move the world.

NAPOLEON BONAPARTE (1769–1821)

Take a Cold Shower

No, NOT for the usual reason . . . but because
cold water triggers our ancient dive reflex. It slows
down our metabolism to protect our body. In turn,
it reduces tension. Negative thoughts often
disappear with the shivers. You're left with a
lovely warm glow, and a new mind-set.

*Winter is on my head but eternal
spring is in my heart.*

VICTOR HUGO (1802–1885)

Call a Friend

WHEN YOU'RE feeling down, don't sit and stew on your own. Talk it over with someone. See or call a good friend or advisor. Sharing the burden always makes it lighter and gives clues to the way ahead.

The antidote for fifty enemies is one friend.

ARISTOTLE (384–322 BC)

Eat Seafood

OR WALNUTS . . . whatever food is rich in omega-3. These fatty acids have many benefits, not least that people with diets rich in them are less likely to suffer from depression. Like most things, these diets aren't a cure, but they contribute to our overall well-being.

One cannot think well, love well, sleep well, if one has not dined well.

VIRGINIA WOOLF (1882–1941)

Re-create Your Strengths

RECALL YOUR most positive moments and
thoughts. Examine how you reached them. Relive
the feelings. Remember them. See how you can
replicate the conditions, and scale the
heights again.

*Example is the school of mankind,
and they will learn at no other.*

EDMUND BURKE (1729–1797)

Host a Dinner

BRING TOGETHER a balanced selection of
friends in a warm convivial location, preferably
your home. Allow the atmosphere to build
naturally. Help to interweave their interests.
Allow the magic to develop.

*Strange to see how a good dinner and
feasting reconciles everybody.*

SAMUEL PEPYS (1633–1703)

Defuse

WHEN FACED with a major problem, talk it
over with someone you trust. Make sure you
identify it accurately. Try to contain your
emotional reaction. Stay in the present when
responding to it. Don't let it grow out
of proportion.

*Never give up, for that is just the place
and time that the tide will turn.*

HARRIET BEECHER STOWE (1811–1896)

Write Your Goals

IT WORKS like a road map. It allows you to locate
your position, and later to check on your progress.
Writing down your goals prompts you to be
specific and crystallizes your thinking.
But you must act to achieve them.

All know the way but few actually walk it.

BODHIDARMA (CA. 500)

Daydream

IT HELPS you to break out of your
bubble. It allows you to explore possibilities,
untrammeled by current problems. It encourages
you to time travel, to enter others' minds,
and to look into the distance.

He does not need opium. He
has the gift of reverie.

ANAÏS NIN (1903–1977)

Play Life's Game

LIFE IS a jigsaw puzzle. You can play only
with the pieces you're given. But you can play it
creatively. The secret lies in seeing the connections.
And that comes from observation and experience.
With time the connections seem obvious.

*Common sense is the realized
sense of proportion.*

MOHANDAS KARAMCHAND "MAHATMA" GANDHI
(1869–1948)

Surrender to Music

CREATE YOUR own music library. Lose yourself in the rhythms. Be transported by the stories and melodies. Music starts where the words stop. Let it wash over you. Surrender to its mysteries.

Music is the universal
language of mankind.

HENRY WADSWORTH LONGFELLOW (1807–1882)

Set Your Own Routine

WE EACH work most effectively at different hours. Some revel at night, some early morning. Find when your mind sparks best. If you can, break out of the nine-to-five strictures. Take control of your timetable. Work your own hours.

Time is what we want most,
but what we use worst.

WILLIAM PENN (1644–1718)

Do What You Love

AND LOVE what you do. Lose yourself in your work. Aim high. Chances are you'll find yourself that way. Trust what inspires you. It will lift you to unexpected heights.

Your work is to discover your work and then with all your heart to give yourself to it.

GAUTAMA BUDDHA (CA. 563–483 BC)

Own Your Happiness

DON'T HITCH your happiness to others. Don't link it to events outside your control. See the distinction between events and your reaction to them. You can control only the latter. Your happiness depends on you.

If you want to be happy, be.

LEO TOLSTOY (1828–1910)

Be a Witness, Not a Judge

WHEN YOU judge, your mind is closed. You
can't learn when you're judgmental. Don't be a
harsh critic of yourself or others. Look for
the positives . . . observe and learn.

*It is the property of fools
to be always judging.*

THOMAS FULLER (1608–1661)

Connect the Dots

OBSERVE THE links, see why people act and
how things work. Watch for the repetitions, see the
patterns. Wisdom is using experience . . . to
understand developing situations
and to solve problems.

To a great mind, nothing is little.

ARTHUR CONAN DOYLE (1859–1930)

Lose the Distractions

IT MAY seem counterintuitive in the digital age, but our world discourages connection. And it militates against deep thinking. Constant mental stimulation distracts. Fight the distractions, and promote your creativity.

This perpetual hurry of business and company ruins me in soul if not in body.

WILLIAM WILBERFORCE (1759–1833)

Use Limits Positively

JUST AS Twitter forces us to be more succinct,
use your limitations positively. Change your mind-
set. View obstacles and borders as opportunities.
Reconstruct the possibilities. Turn your
thoughts into things.

*Some people grumble that roses have
thorns; I am grateful that thorns
have roses.*

JEAN-BAPTISTE ALPHONSE KARR (1808–1890)

Find Your Heritage

IT LIES in the stories of your family and your
tribe. But look behind the stories for the truth.
Many were imperfect when handed down, or were
pure fabrications. You may choose how heritage
influences you, but it will explain many things.

*Commonly men will only be brave as their
fathers were brave, or timid.*

HENRY DAVID THOREAU (1817–1862)

Get a Massage

NOT ONLY is massage a wonderful way to lose tension, it boosts our mood. It reduces our levels of cortisol, the stress hormone. It promotes feelings of well-being. It counteracts the impact of sitting all day. It helps you sleep.

There is more wisdom in your body than in your deepest philosophies.

FRIEDRICH NIETZSCHE (1844–1900)

Go to the Source

WHETHER IT'S via Google or the library, always seek primary sources. Beware of secondhand views or conclusions, especially those online, dressed as expert doctrine. Keep asking questions. And insist on finding the answers yourself.

Research is the highest form of adoration.

PIERRE TEILHARD DE CHARDIN, SJ (1881–1955)

Use It

NOTICE HOW nature takes back anything
not used? It's the same with our bodies,
our minds, even our freedom or our democracy.
It's up to us to make sure we keep both
active. And the more we exercise our minds
and bodies, the more they reward us.

*The most difficult thing is the decision to
act, the rest is merely tenacity.*

AMELIA EARHART (1897–1937)

Smile Your Eyes

A SIMPLE smile has immense power. It transforms your aura. It warms a room. It can even change a life. Smiling your eyes drives tension from your face, and invites a mirrored response.

A smile recures the wounding of a frown.

WILLIAM SHAKESPEARE (1564–1616)

Enjoy Your Own Company

SOLITUDE IS your chance to refuel. Take
advantage of spare moments. Allow your
imagination to fly free. Enjoy the rejuvenating
quietness, the chance to refine your soul,
and to reflect without pressure.

*The worst loneliness is not to be
comfortable with yourself.*

MARK TWAIN (SAMUEL LANGHORNE CLEMENS)
(1835–1910)

Open the Windows

FEEL THE breeze, and the fresh air as it brings renewal. Watch the light fill the rooms. Listen to the sounds of the street, breathe in the new day, open up to new ideas.

A house without books is like a room without windows.

HORACE MANN (1796–1859)

Rearrange the Furniture

IT'S A great way to change perspective, to look
anew at your home or office. It will prompt you to
clean unseen areas. It will open new options. It will
galvanize your creative eye and lead to a
refreshed environment.

*Those who cannot change their minds
cannot change anything.*

GEORGE BERNARD SHAW (1856–1950)

Blossom Like a Flower

GROW WITH slow purpose, in harmony, and
in your time. Grow through your inner strength,
sustained by the power of your spirit.
And, at the right time, bloom.

*Every flower is a soul blossoming
in nature.*

GÉRARD DE NERVAL (GÉRARD LABRUNIE)
(1808–1855)

Cradle a Baby

IT BRINGS an immediate connection like no other, heart straight to heart, as the miracle of life is personified. The unique scent of infant innocence, the aura of trusting helplessness, all redolent of unlimited potential.

Life is a flame that is always burning itself out, but it catches fire again every time a child is born.

GEORGE BERNARD SHAW (1856–1950)

The Best Is Yet to Come

THE REST of your life . . . should be the best of your life. You have the power to make it so. Look up and ahead: remember, whatever stage you're at . . . it's not your final destination.

There is no end. There is no beginning.
There is only the infinite passion of life.

FEDERICO FELLINI (1920–1993)

Meet Your Hero

YOU MAY be setting yourself up for
disappointment. Your heroes may have feet of
stone. But maybe that's not really important. It's
what they mean to you, what they stand for, and
what they inspire in you, that makes
them important.

*As you get older is it is harder to have
heroes, but it is sort of necessary.*

ERNEST HEMINGWAY (1899–1961)

Credit the Effort

CHANGE YOUR focus. Give credit to yourself
and others, and especially your kids, for the effort,
not just the successes. It will inspire them
to greater heights.

*When you cannot get a compliment in
any other way pay yourself one.*

MARK TWAIN (SAMUEL LANGHORNE CLEMENS)
(1835–1910)

Embrace Your Potential

WE ALL have untapped potential. It lies within us awaiting our call. Its greatest enemy is often fear, or lack of confidence. The only thing preventing us from reaching it . . . is us.

If you hear a voice within you say "you cannot paint," then by all means paint, and that voice will be silenced.

VINCENT VAN GOGH (1853 –1890)

Get in the Zone

SPORTS CHAMPIONS aim to play "in the zone."
There they transcend conscious thought, to play
instinctively at their optimal level. We can do it by
immersing ourselves in work we love, which
inspires us so much that we lose track of time.

*The most powerful weapon on
earth is the human soul on fire.*

FERDINAND FOCH (1851–1929)

Take a Small Step

STAGING IS the secret to so many things. At first
view many goals are enormous. Some simply
appear unachievable. But divide them into smaller
sections, stages that can be easily envisaged,
and you'll transform the journey.

Progress is not accomplished in one stage.

VICTOR HUGO (1802–1885)

Pause on a Roll

IT'S TEMPTING to go hard on any task, until you're exhausted. But it's much smarter to take a break, while you still have something in the tank. That way, when you resume, you can power on from where you left off.

*It does not matter how slowly you go
as long as you do not stop.*

CONFUCIUS (551–479 BC)

Join Your Head to Your Heart

AIM TO align your values and your actions.
Happiness lies there. Interweave your heart and
your mind. Consider it a work in progress. Don't
look for perfection. Instead, concentrate
on the effort.

*One ought to hold on to one's heart; for if
one lets it go, one soon loses control
of the head too.*

FRIEDRICH NIETZSCHE (1844–1900)

Find the Trade-Offs

LIFE IS rarely definitive. Usually it's a series
of compromises between desires and possibilities,
hopes and realities, achievements and
fulfillment. Seek fulfillment.

*Compromise is the best and
cheapest lawyer.*

ROBERT LOUIS STEVENSON (1850–1894)

Read Every Day

FICTION OR nonfiction, book or tablet. It's not about the package, it's about the ideas. Great fiction will inspire, transport you, open your mind and heart. Great nonfiction will inform and broaden your world.

I guess there are never enough books.

JOHN STEINBECK (1902–1968)

Tell Stories

ESPECIALLY TELL your unique tales. People
will learn more about you. You'll learn more about
yourself. Your stories validate your life choices.
They explain your history. They bring you
and your listeners closer.

*If history were taught in the form of
stories, it would never be forgotten.*

RUDYARD KIPLING (1865–1936)

Chat with Strangers

SURE, PICK your time and the person, but trust your instinct. Connect with your eyes, open your heart. It's amazing what you'll learn. You'll spread warmth and confirm humanity.

There are no strangers here; only friends you haven't met yet.

WILLIAM BUTLER YEATS (1865–1939)

Appreciate Success

ESPECIALLY THE success of others. It's easy to
feel jealous, and begrudge them their achievements.
But most are being rewarded for their hard work.
Use it as an example. Follow in their
footsteps and beyond.

Life is too short to be little.

BENJAMIN DISRAELI (1804–1881)

Treasure Your Humanity

DON'T TAKE it for granted. Value it in yourself
and in others. Fight to retain and foster it. Allow
your real feelings to reign. Let them steer you
toward the beautiful things in life.

*We are healthy only to the extent
that our ideas are humane.*

KURT VONNEGUT (1922–2007)

Speak the Truth

IT CAN require great courage. And it's often the hard path, especially when it shows you in a bad light, or as the one against the crowd. But have it as your aim, or you'll find yourself replaying lost opportunities.

Be truthful, gentle, and fearless.

MOHANDAS KARAMCHAND "MAHATMA" GANDHI

(1869–1948)

Ignore the Shortcut

IT'S SO tempting to cut corners. But often it ends up being destructive. Take the time. Do it right. Do the hard work. Reap the full reward.

Act as if what you do makes a difference. It does.

WILLIAM JAMES (1842–1910)

Ask for Help

VERY FEW things are done better alone. And
team achievements are invariably sweeter. Asking
for help reminds people of their value. It's a
compliment, a sign of respect. But do it to their
timetable. And give them their credit.

*It is one of the most beautiful
compensations of this life that no man
can sincerely try to help another
without helping himself.*

RALPH WALDO EMERSON (1803–1882)

Try Differently

IF IT'S not working, simple repetition
won't solve it. Pause, reassess, look at the problem
anew. Before trying again, or trying harder,
look from a different angle. Then try it smarter,
and do it differently.

*The only way to avoid making mistakes
is to have no new ideas.*

ALBERT EINSTEIN (1879–1955)

Give Yourself

WHETHER IT'S your time, your heart, or your money. It's a scientifically proven fact, showing kindness to others, helping them in almost any way, brings an immediate increase . . .
in your well-being.

For it is in giving that we receive.

FRANCIS OF ASSISI (1181–1226)

Plan a Journey

THE STRANGE thing is . . . you don't actually
have to take the trip. Just start making plans for it.
The anticipation of planning your journey boosts
your happiness levels for many weeks.

*The real voyage of discovery consists not
in seeking new landscapes, but in
having new eyes.*

MARCEL PROUST (1871–1922)

Value Your Down Time

ESPECIALLY AS you get older, relaxation time is
far more valuable than money. It returns so many
more benefits, to your family, your health,
your happiness.

*Take rest; a field that has rested
gives a bountiful crop.*

OVID (43 BC–AD 17)

You're Not Your Work

YOUR WORK doesn't measure your worth.
It shouldn't define you to others or to yourself.
Your work won't last forever. Don't let it dominate
your views or your lifestyle.

What the superior man seeks is in himself;
what the small man seeks is in others.

CONFUCIUS (551–479 BC)

Break Out of Busy

WE'RE BUSY most of the time. But don't let it become an excuse to procrastinate. Successful busy people find the time to deal with their work, to be with their families and loved ones, and to care for their health.

It's not enough to be busy, so are the ants.
The question is, what are we busy about.

HENRY DAVID THOREAU (1817–1862)

Review the Facts

WHEN EMOTIONS run high and things threaten to get out of hand, mentally step back and take yourself out of the picture. Revert to the facts. Argue and choose purely on those facts.

Evolution is a light that illuminates all facts, a curve that all lines must follow.

PIERRE TEILHARD DE CHARDIN, SJ (1881–1955)

Retain Your Power

NO MATTER how great the pressure, or how confused the situation, hold tight to your personal power of choice. You always have the final say, to make your own choices, according to your own beliefs.

Life is the sum of all your choices.

ALBERT CAMUS (1913–1960)

Focus on Others

IN THE end, it's not about you. In fact, there's
you . . . and the rest of the world is others.
The more you turn your attention away from
yourself, the more you open your heart,
the more your mind will follow.

*True humility is not thinking less of
yourself, it is thinking of yourself less.*

C. S. LEWIS (1898–1963)